Moments

Zahara Razzaq

Presentation by *BookLeaf Publishing*

Web: www.bookleafpub.com

E-mail: info@bookleafpub.com

ISBN: 978-93-5761-085-8

First edition 2022

DEDICATION

To my amazing family, friends and colleagues - thank you for being my inspiration today and always!

A Start

A cool breeze
The sun shines
A new month
Nature thrives

A chapter of hope
People smile
Flowers bloom
No room for gloom

The strength within
Keep up that chin
Catch your breath
Take the step

Share your smile
This is the start

Memories of You

The warmth of your touch
The dimples in your cheek
An everlasting smile
An untouched memory

Your contagious laugh
Your outspoken voice
A colourful mind
The home that I found

For Me

When the goal is achieved
It is for no one but me
Because above all else
It's not what others see
It's who I'm destined to be

A Promise

My promise to you
This pain won't last forever
I await the day your smile reaches your eyes
And for all the laughter lines to reappear

And whilst I have you here with me now
I'll make the most of this time
To tell you to never stop believing
And to always embrace that hopeful feeling

Ready?

But, my darling, don't you know?
This is your breakthrough

A Poignant Moment

The room is filled with her presence
She exudes the essence of life
Lying in a cloud of comfort
She whispers her last words

Her family nestle beside her
A sombre silence ensues
Grief engulfs them
As a thunderstorm awakens

The shock is replaced by heartfelt tears
And the promise of sunlight returns
A colourful rainbow forms outside
As a beacon of hope and grace

The troubled world awakens
As a new dawn rises
In all endings
There is the beauty of a new beginning

In the stillness of life
Never lose hope
For this life is unpredictable
And yet there is much to come

Battlefield

7

Their scars alight in the blazing sun
Colourful wildflowers in a sea of green
A sharp breeze cut through the trees
Faces of loved ones haunting their minds
Homebound to civilisation

The unexpected return
The patriotic salute
Medals of honour
Like unforgotten memories

Newborn

With skin so soft
And eyes like jewels
Your lips curl into a smile
And the intrepid pain dissipates
All words are lost
Time stands still
Long enough to say…
Welcome to the world, little one
You are forever loved

Step outside

Feel the warmth of the sun on your skin
Take a long, deep breath
Let the softness of the grass cushion your feet
Feel the tingle in your bones
Close your tired eyes
Take a bow
You are alive

Infected

Such joy there is in laughter
For one smile is contagious
So I direct my words at you today
Share your smile and let the world be infected

Round and Round

11

An automatic high
A constant change
A black hole
A merry go round
This is the circle of life

Warrior

Her love was a token
Of loyalty unspoken
Her heart torn to pieces
Her skin creases

A soul that ached
For a love that was faked
Crystal tears
Shed from her fears

She stood up tall
And heard her heart call
Her feet grounded
And then she pounded

The beat of life
In a world of strife
Unspoken words
She escaped like the birds

Free from captivity
Soaring into activity
She dazzled like the stars
With embellished scars

Child of the Sun

Behold the sun
Chase it for fun
Let the warmth engulf you
As it enriches you too

Love

Lights up your life, and
Opens your heart, to
Victorious feelings, with
Endless seasonings

No Regrets

15

Treat me with compassion
And I will gracefully accept
Act now with kindness
And I will share your joy
Take the unseen risk
And live with no regrets

Endings

Memories like gold
They could never get old
But then you turned cold
And it all started to fold

And now they turn to rust
With sprinkles of dust
Familiar love changed to lust
With behaviours that are unjust

We walk away
Like strangers who must pay
Nothing left to say
Come what may

This is the end
I can no longer pretend
All that I defend
I cannot amend

The Boy

17

Hearts flutter
No more clutter
A sparkling life
Laughter is rife
This moment is joy
Here comes the boy

One Night

Engulfed in darkness
An ensuing madness
The hollow weeping
And silent screaming

Rise

Be like the phoenix
Grow from the ashes
Alight your soul
Unleash your voice

Trust Yourself

20

Let. It. Go.
Close the door.

Release

21

Whisper thank you for what has passed
It is the end
Appreciate the gift of the present
Here you are now
Remain open to what's coming
Its an unknown surprise

www.ingramcontent.com/pod-product-compliance
Lightning Source LLC
LaVergne TN
LVHW051248200726